Reflect

Reflect

Haikus for Worship

Stephanie Mathews

RESOURCE *Publications* • Eugene, Oregon

REFLECT

Copyright © 2022 Stephanie Mathews. All rights reserved. Except for brief quotations in critical publications or reviews, no part of this book may be reproduced in any manner without prior written permission from the publisher. Write: Permissions, Wipf and Stock Publishers, 199 W. 8th Ave., Suite 3, Eugene, OR 97401.

Resource Publications
An Imprint of Wipf and Stock Publishers
199 W. 8th Ave., Suite 3
Eugene, OR 97401

www.wipfandstock.com

PAPERBACK ISBN: 978-1-6667-4503-0
HARDCOVER ISBN: 978-1-6667-4504-7
EBOOK ISBN: 978-1-6667-4505-4

JUNE 10, 2022 8:12 AM

Contents

The Name	1
Provision	2
The Shepherd	3
True Love	4
The Peace	5
Healing	6
The Banner	7
Almighty	8
El Roi	9
Goodness	10
Holy, Holy, Holy	11
Venerate	12
The Dove	13
The Creator	14
The Artist	15
Constellations	16
Most High	17
Handiwork	18
The Word	19
Universal	20

Limitless	21
Endless	22
Great God	23
The Love	24
God Eternal	25
The Christ	26
All Knowing	27
God Said	28
Mastermind	29
The Water	30
The Lord	31
Mercy	32
The Truth	33
Vengeance	34
The Judge	35
Living God	36
The Way	37
The Last Adam	38
Salvation	39
Trust	40
My Strength	41
The Burden	42
Faithful	43
Deliverance	44

Forever	45
Redemption	46
Risen	47
Seek	48
New Life	49
The Gift	50
The Gospel	51
The Savior	52
Wickedness	53
Agony	54
The Debt	55
Repentance	56
Blindness	57
Redemption	58
With Us	59
The Comfort	60
The Fruit	61
The Cross	62
Cursed	63
His Children	64
The Likeness	65
The Prince	66
The King	67
Everything	68

The Name

YHWH is the name
All existence comes from Him
He is creator

Provision

Jehovah-Jira
The creator will provide
Alive is His word

The Shepherd

The good shepherd is
The lamb, the lion, the Lord
God the redeemer

True Love

True love is patient
True love is kind and bears all
God radiates love

The Peace

Jehovah-Shalom
The Lord has given us peace
Let us rest in Him

Healing

The Lord brings healing
Jehovah-Rophe brings life
Partake and be well

The Banner

Jehovah-Nissi
The Lord God is my banner
I will lift His name

Almighty

El Shaddai is He
Almighty is he who came
To lay down his life

El Roi

He's the God who sees
All that is on the inside
He sees outside too

Goodness

God is truth and love
God is merciful and just
He is all goodness

Holy, Holy, Holy

Majestic is God
Majesty to our Lord God
The angels do sing

Venerate

Reverence to God
Our veneration to Him
Bless his holy name

The Dove

The Holy Spirit
A dove that comes from heaven
To dwell in our hearts

The Creator

He spoke and light came
The beginning God did make
He created all

The Artist

He spoke and life was
The universe displays it
Everyone will see

Constellations

It's written up high
The stars tell of a story
The heavens declare

Most High

O' El Elyon
The One who is everything
Look to God Most High

Handiwork

Creation displays
The firmament shows design
His handiwork seen

The Word

The Living Word Came
The Word became flesh for us
The Word is the way

Universal

He is everywhere
The Lord is omnipresent
He dwells in all space

Limitless

God is infinite
His ways are beyond measure
God is limitless

Endless

Everlasting God
No beginning or ending
God everlasting

Great God

The great Elohim
He is strength, power, and might
Behold His glory

The Love

God is the great love
Love that came and walked with us
The love in plain sight

God Eternal

In the beginning
God eternal was present
And always will be

The Christ

The angels appeared
Announcing to the shepherds
Immanuel born

All Knowing

He is omniscient
He knows all things that will be
He is pansophic

God Said

God said and it was
Everything made by His power
Sovereignty is God

Mastermind

Magnificent plan
All the details perfected
God takes care of all

The Water

The Living Water
Is He who came down to us
Offering the truth

The Lord

God is Adonai
His reign is everlasting
He is Lord of all

Mercy

God is full of grace
That dead in sins He still saves
His mercy is great

The Truth

He can save us all
The truth made available
Believe in the truth

Vengeance

Judgment is for God
Trust in His perfect justice
For vengeance is God's

The Judge

God is the great judge
All deeds to be on trial
At the judgment seat

Living God

Elohim Chayim
His reign will be forever
The true Living God

The Way

God gave us the law
To show the right way to live
Jesus is the way

The Last Adam

The first Adam sinned
Now everyone is condemned
The last Adam saves

Salvation

By one man came death
God became man to save us
Salvation by Him

Trust

Sample and see Him
Blessed are those who believe it
Fear the Lord and live

My Strength

Mighty in power
All my strength comes from the Lord
His Word holds me up

The Burden

The burden is big
It can't be carried alone
Jesus carries it

Faithful

His covenants kept
God's faithfulness is the hope
To not die again

Deliverance

Sin is infection
The cross is what will heal
Releasing from sin

Forever

Pardon is needed
To not die a second death
Forever with God

Redemption

Sin stains our spirit
Nothing will wash it away
But the blood of Christ

Risen

Graced are you who see
The miracle from the cross
Jesus is risen

Seek

There is more to life
Then desires with our flesh
Seek the One who saves

New Life

All we have is life
Belief is being alive
Be alive and have new life

The Gift

The Lord has paid it
The price for eternal life
A gift freely gave

The Gospel

The good news is here
Share what brings eternal life
God wants all to live

The Savior

We are born in sin
The wrath of God awaits all
Jesus Christ alive

Wickedness

Wrath is due to all
Wickedness will be punished
Turn away from sin

Agony

To be separate
From God is hell and true death
Grief unbearable

The Debt

The law will condemn
It cries out for what is due
All debts collected

Repentance

Wrong will be punished
Jesus came and paid the price
Repent and believe

Blindness

He has given life
Yet all rebel against Him
Help the truth be seen

Redemption

The gospel is news
Good news that God became flesh
Saving us from death

With Us

From heaven He came
Messiah with his people
The Creator God

The Comfort

The Holy Spirit
The solace, the peace, the joy
To dwell within us

The Fruit

Fruit of the Spirit
Will bear on those who believe
Planted in the truth

The Cross

The cross brings us close
Our good works are dirty rags
Only God is good

Cursed

The earth cursed with thorns
Jesus' head crowned with thorns
Our curse put on Him

His Children

To be like children
Those will enter the kingdom
To commune with God

The Likeness

We have a standard
Imago Dei we are made
We bear His image

The Prince

He is Prince of Peace
Born to save all creation
The enemy crushed

The King

Return of the King
The second coming brings Him
Return in power

Everything

I AM the alpha
The beginning and the end
I AM Omega

www.ingramcontent.com/pod-product-compliance
Lightning Source LLC
Chambersburg PA
CBHW071743040426
42446CB00012B/2451